Mel Bay Presents

Hymn Tunes

for Unaccompanied Violin

by Marilyn Carlson

1 2 3 4 5 6 7 8 9 0

© 2005 BY MEL BAY PUBLICATIONS, INC., PACIFIC, MO 63069.
ALL RIGHTS RESERVED. INTERNATIONAL COPYRIGHT SECURED. B.M.I. MADE AND PRINTED IN U.S.A.
No part of this publication may be reproduced in whole or in part, or stored in a retrieval system, or transmitted in any form
or by any means, electronic, mechanical, photocopy, recording, or otherwise, without written permission of the publisher.

Visit us on the Web at www.melbay.com — E-mail us at email@melbay.com

Come, Thou Fount of Every Blessing 5

Amazing Grace 6

Come, Ye Sinners, Poor and Needy 8

When I Survey the Wondrous Cross 9

Jesus Paid It All 10

Lord, Enthroned in Heavenly Splendor 12

My Faith Looks Up to Thee 14

Jesus, Lover of My Soul 16

This World Is Not My Home 18

Coventry Carol 20

Sweet Little Jesus Boy 22

What Wondrous Love (Fantasia for Unaccompanied Violin) 24

About the Author 29

This page has been left blank to avoid awkward page turns

Come, Thou Fount of Every Blessing

NETTLETON
John Wyeth
arr. by Marilyn Carlson

Amazing Grace

NEW BRITAIN
19th century American melody
arr. by Marilyn Carlson

Come, Ye Sinners, Poor and Needy

ARISE
Traditional American Melody
arr. by Marilyn Carlson

When I Survey the Wondrous Cross

HAMBURG
Lowell Mason
arr. by Marilyn Carlson

Jesus Paid It All

ALL TO CHRIST
John T. Grape
arr. by Marilyn Carlson

Lord, Enthroned in Heavenly Splendor

BRYN CALFARIA
William Owen
arr. by Marilyn Carlson

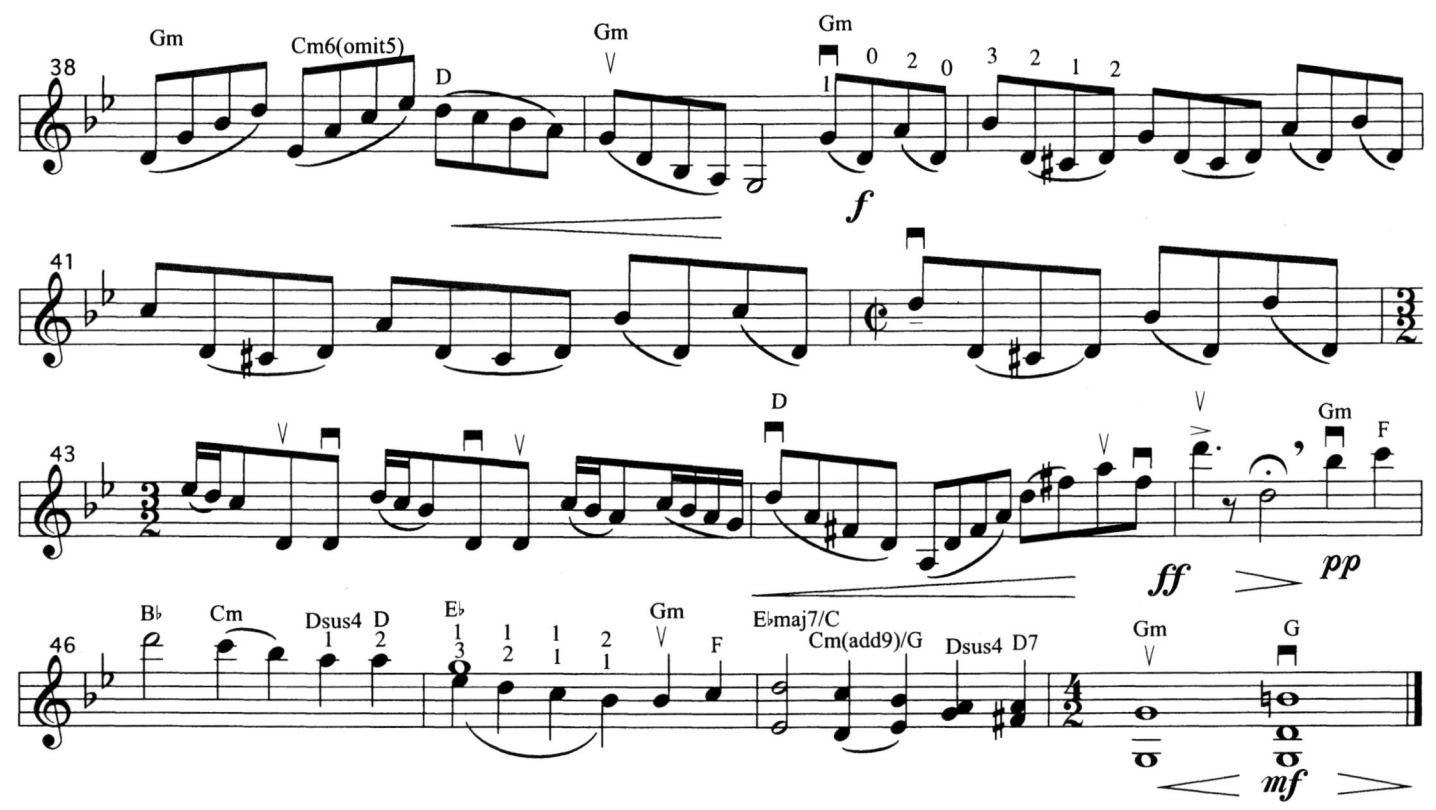

13

My Faith Looks Up to Thee

OLIVET
Lowell Mason
arr. by Marilyn Carlson

Jesus, Lover of My Soul

MARTYN
Simeon B. Marsh
arr. by Marilyn Carlson

This World Is Not My Home

Traditional
arr. by Marilyn Carlson

Coventry Carol

COVENTRY CAROL
melody from *Pageant of the Shearmen and Tailors*, 15th cent.
arr. by Marilyn Carlson

Sweet Little Jesus Boy

Traditional
arr. by Marilyn Carlson

What Wondrous Love
Fantasia for Unaccompanied Violin

WONDROUS LOVE
melody in William Walker's
Southern Harmony, 1835
arr. by Marilyn Carlson

About the Author

Marilyn Carlson is a native of Seattle, Washington and was raised in a musical home. Starting piano at the age of 6 and violin at the age of 9, she played in school and community orchestras while growing up. She holds degrees in math and librarianship and is employed at the University of Washington Medical Center. Marilyn is active in musical ministry in churches, nursing homes, and retirement communities, and has written a variety of music for use in these settings. Her publications include hymn arrangements for violin, viola, cello, violin trio, string quartet, and flute.